WELL-TEMPERED PRAISE III

Piano Arrangements
by
Mark Hayes

Cover Illustration Paul Wolf
Graphic Designer John Clarke Summers

HE5034

EXCLUSIVELY DISTRIBUTED BY

HAL•LEONARD® CORPORATION
7777 W. BLUEMOUND RD. P.O. BOX 13819 MILWAUKEE, WI 53213

CONTENTS

PERFORMANCE NOTES

SING TO THE LORD is a contemporary Christian standard popularized by Sandi Patti. Energy, combined with a rock-steady tempo and good, clean articulation are the key words here. There is a very wide range of dynamics, so make the most of them.

THE LIGHT OF THE WORLD IS JESUS should be played rather unassumingly with interest coming from the rhythmic variances and the fresh harmonies. Be sure to shape and phrase the melody.

SIMPLE GIFTS is one of my favorite American folk tunes. I've tried to capture a simple, dance-like feel with Appalachian idioms much like Copland did. Take care to play the first 15 bars with as much musicianship as the rest of the arrangement.

I NEED THEE EVERY HOUR is a hymn tune that I often find myself playing in my own personal devotions. I decided to set it in 4/4 meter and in a minor key to heighten the emotion of the text. Don't be in a hurry on the second page. The 16th note section was written as a fantasia or development section and should be played freely and from the heart.

SHALL WE GATHER AT THE RIVER/NEAR TO THE HEART OF GOD were coupled because of the connection between the heavenly throne of God and "a place of quiet rest near to the heart of God." Play this arrangement peacefully but "milk" all those wonderful altered harmonies. You should have your audience weeping at the end.

FOR UNTO US A CHILD IS BORN. There is nothing like Handel for good energetic playing. Pay special attention to articulation and dynamics throughout. Play cleanly and pedal sparingly.

JOYSONG is one of my newest piano compositions. It is simply meant to evoke joy to the listener's ear. As with many of my pieces, it is quite syncopated in nature so take care to play rhythms properly. It is lighthearted and delicate on the whole and will work just as well at a tempo slower than $\quarternote = 168$ if necessary.

JOSHUA FIT THE BATTLE OF JERICHO demonstrates my penchant for jazz and has never failed to be a crowd-pleaser wherever it has been performed. Don't be in a hurry and be sure to get into the "swing" of it, paying careful attention to accents placed on the off beats.

PEOPLE NEED THE LORD is a wonderful "heart" song that was popularized by Christian singer Steve Green. I've tried to create the same poignancy in this arrangement that is evoked by the text. Play it slowly with care, paying attention to what notes are the melody and what notes are not in the first chorus. Feel free to embellish the arpeggio seven bars from the end.

PRAISE HIS GREATNESS is a medley of the hymn tune "HYFRYDOL" and the contemporary hymn, GREAT IS THE LORD, by Michael W. Smith. Maintain the same tempo if possible throughout, gauging how fast you should start by how fast you can play the hardest section with accuracy. Be sure and project the melody at the introduction of each new theme, which is indicated by either accents or up stems.

Mark Hayes

SING TO THE LORD

Words and Music by
Robert Sterling
Arr. by **MARK HAYES**

THE LIGHT OF THE WORLD IS JESUS

Words and Music by Philip P. Bliss
Arr. by MARK HAYES

Flowing (♩ = 132)

SIMPLE GIFTS

Traditional Shaker Melody
Arr. by **MARK HAYES**

I NEED THEE EVERY HOUR

Words by
Annie S. Hawks

Music: NEED
Robert Lowry
Arr. by MARK HAYES

SHALL WE GATHER AT THE RIVER
NEAR TO THE HEART OF GOD

Arr. by **MARK HAYES**

* *Words and Music by* Robert Lowry

NEAR TO THE HEART OF GOD*

L.H.   R.H.

Words and Music by Cleland McAfee

SHALL WE GATHER AT THE RIVER

This page has been left blank intentionally
in order to avoid awkward page turns.

FOR UNTO US A CHILD IS BORN

G.F. Handel
Arr. by **MARK HAYES**

JOY SONG

MARK HAYES

Well-articulated, with a steady tempo (♩ = 168)

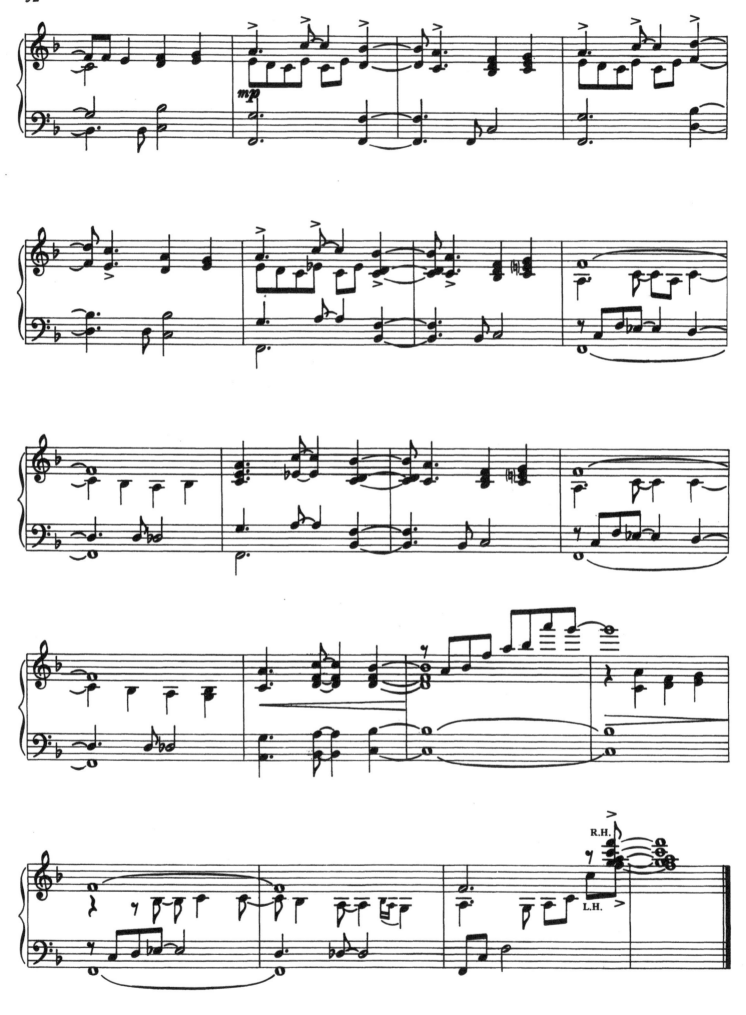

*This page has been left blank intentionally
in order to avoid awkward page turns.*

JOSHUA FIT THE BATTLE OF JERICHO

Spiritual
Arr by MARK HAYES

PEOPLE NEED THE LORD

Words and Music by
Phill McHugh *and* **Greg Nelson**
Arr by **MARK HAYES**

Slowly, with feeling

PRAISE HIS GREATNESS

Arr by **MARK HAYES**

* *Music by* Rowland Hugh Prichard

GREAT IS THE LORD*

bring out melody